Essential Guide to Writing

Writing Avenue

Rachel Somer

Paragraph Writing

1

DARAKWON

About the Author

Rachel Somer

BA in English Literature, York University, Toronto, Canada

Award-winning essayist, TOEIC developer, and author of educational books

Over ten years of experience as an English as a Second Language instructor

The author of *Fundamental Reading* Basic 1 and 2

Essential Guide to Writing

Writing Avenue 1
Paragraph Writing

Publisher Chung Kyudo
Author Rachel Somer
Editors Jeong Yeonsoon, Kim Mina, Seo Jeong-ah, Kim Mikyeong
Designers Park Narae, Forest

First published in February 2021
By Darakwon, Inc.
Darakwon Bldg., 211, Munbal-ro, Paju-si, Gyeonggi-do 10881
Republic of Korea
Tel: 82-2-736-2031 (Ext. 250)
Fax: 82-2-732-2037

Copyright © 2021 Darakwon, Inc.

ISBN 978-89-277-0447-8 54740
978-89-277-0446-1 54740 (set)

www.darakwon.co.kr

Photo Credits
muzsy (p. 27), marcobrivio.photo (p. 62), Bumble Dee (p. 64), Anticiclo (p. 64), Zhao jiankang (p. 64) / www.shutterstock.com

Components Main Book / Workbook
10 9 8 7 6 5 4   23 24 25 26 27

Essential Guide to Writing

Writing Avenue

Paragraph Writing

1

Table of Contents

Table of Contents

How to Use This Book

• Student Book

1. Before You Write

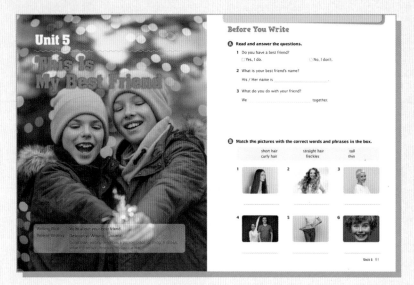

Thinking about the Topic

Three warm-up questions help students think about the writing topic.

Previewing the Key Vocabulary

Students can learn the key vocabulary by matching the words with the pictures or filling in the table.

2. Understanding the Model Text

QR code for listening to the model text

Reading the Model Text

Students can read an example of the writing topic and use it as a template when they write their passage.

Completing the Graphic Organizer

By completing the graphic organizer, students can learn the structure of the model text. This also helps them organize their writing.

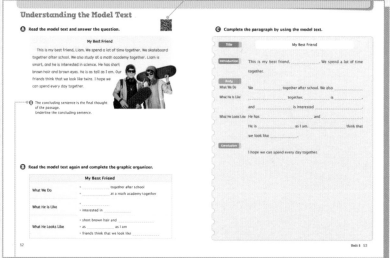

A question about the model text is provided.

Completing the Paragraph

By completing the paragraph, students can review the model text and learn what the passage consists of.

3. Collecting Ideas

Getting Ideas from Collecting Ideas

Ideas related to the writing topic are provided. Students can brainstorm and learn new ideas before writing their draft.

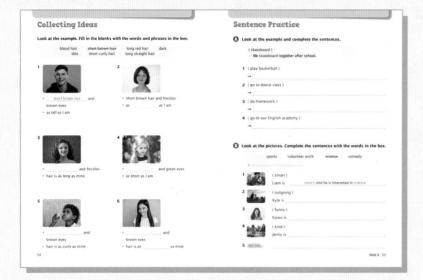

4. Sentence Practice

Practicing Sentences with Key Structures

Various types of questions allow students to practice the key structures of the model text. They also help students gather ideas before writing.

5. Sentence Practice Plus

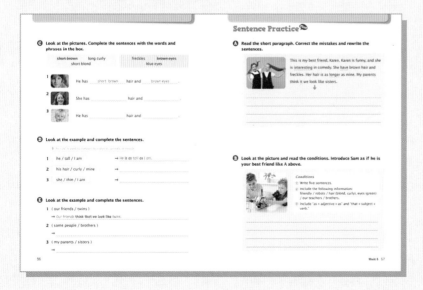

Correcting a Short Paragraph

Students can check if they understand the key structures they learned by correcting the mistakes in the short paragraph.

Writing a Short Paragraph

Students should write a short paragraph by using the given picture and the conditions. This helps students practice the key structures.

6. Brainstorming & First Draft

Brainstorming

By completing the graphic organizer, students can organize their ideas prior to writing the first draft.

First Draft

Students should complete the first draft by using the graphic organizer. They can revise, edit the first draft, and write the final draft in the workbook.

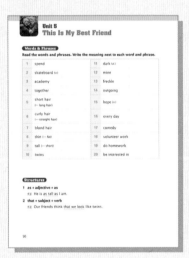

Vocabulary and Structure Review

Students can review the key vocabulary they learned in each unit by writing the meaning of each word and phrase. They can also review the key structures in the unit.

• *Workbook*

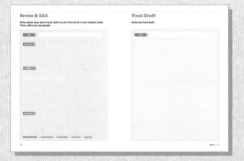

7. More Questions

Students can practice and review the key structures. They can also complete the model text by matching the phrases.

8. Revise & Edit ➜ Final Draft

After writing the first draft, students can revise and edit the draft, and then write the final draft.

About Paragraph Writing

1. What Is a Paragraph?

A paragraph is a short piece of writing that handles a single idea or concept. All the sentences in a given paragraph should be related to a single topic. Paragraphs can stand alone, or they can be added to longer pieces of writing such as essays, stories, articles, and many more.

2. What Does a Paragraph Consist of?

A paragraph consists of a topic sentence, supporting details, and a concluding sentence.

– The topic sentence is the main idea of the passage.

– Supporting details are information and examples that explain the topic.

– The concluding sentence is the final thought of the passage.

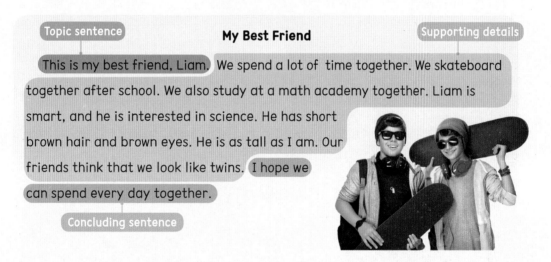

My Best Friend

Topic sentence

Supporting details

This is my best friend, Liam. We spend a lot of time together. We skateboard together after school. We also study at a math academy together. Liam is smart, and he is interested in science. He has short brown hair and brown eyes. He is as tall as I am. Our friends think that we look like twins. I hope we can spend every day together.

Concluding sentence

3. What Are the Types of Paragraph Writing?

1) Expository Writing

It gives information about a topic or tells you how to do something.

2) Narrative Writing

It describes a story that happened to you. It can also describe imaginary events.

3) Persuasive Writing

It encourages a reader to make a choice by providing evidence and examples.

4) Descriptive Writing

It describes a person, place, or thing. It shows what the person, location, or object is like.

Unit 1

Let Me Introduce Myself

Writing Goal	Write about yourself.
Type of Writing	Expository Writing » Presentation
	Expository writing gives information about a topic or tells you how to do something.

Before You Write

A **Read and answer the questions.**

1 What is your name?

My name is _____ .

2 How old are you?

I'm _____ years old.

3 What grade are you in?

I'm in the _____ grade.

B **Match the pictures with the correct words and phrases in the box.**

comic books   my dog   pictures
tennis   video games   model airplanes

1

play with _____

2

make _____

3

play _____

4

draw _____

5

read _____

6

play _____

Understanding the Model Text

A **Read the model text and answer the question.**

My Name Is Jessica Park

Hello, let me introduce myself. My name is Jessica Park. I'm 12 years old, and I live in Toronto. I'm in the sixth grade at Johnson Elementary School. I like to play with my dog and draw pictures in my free time. I also love to play video games. My favorite subject is art. I want to be a video game designer. I want to make my own games someday. Thank you for listening.

Q The topic sentence is the main idea of the passage. Underline the topic sentence.

B **Read the model text again and complete the graphic organizer.**

Jessica Park	
Age and Grade	• _____ old • in the _____ grade _____ Johnson Elementary School
My Hobbies	• _____ with my dog • _____ pictures • play _____
My Favorite Subject	_____
My Dream	• want to be _____ • want to make my _____

C **Complete the paragraph by using the model text.**

My Name Is Jessica Park

Introduction

Hello, let me _____ myself.

Body

Age

My name is _____ . I'm _____ old, and I live

Grade

_____ . I'm _____ grade at _____

My Hobbies

_____ School. I like to _____ and

_____ in my free time. I also love to _____

My Favorite Subject

_____ . My favorite subject is _____ . I want to

My Dream

be _____ . I want to _____

someday.

Conclusion

Thank you for listening.

Collecting Ideas

Look at the example. Fill in the blanks with the phrases in the box.

an athlete	~~draw pictures~~	play board games
go to Mars	ride my bike	a video game designer

My Hobbies

1

- play with my dog
- <u>draw pictures</u>

2

- _____
- make model airplanes

3

- read comic books
- _____

My Dream

4

- _____
- make my own games

5

- an astronaut
- _____

6

- _____
- go to the Olympics

Sentence Practice

A **Look at the pictures and complete the sentences.**

💡 Use "first, second, third, fourth, fifth, or sixth" when writing about your grade.

1 I'm in the sixth grade at _____ Johnson Elementary School.

2 _____ Oak Elementary School.

3 _____ West Elementary School.

4 _____ Baker Middle School.

5 Your Idea _____

B **Look at the example and complete the sentences.**

1 (play with my dog / draw pictures)

→ **I like to** play with my dog **and** draw pictures. _____

2 (ride my bike / make model airplanes)

→ _____

3 (read comic books / play board games)

→ _____

4 (watch movies / bake cookies)

→ _____

Your Idea

5 _____

C Look at the example and complete the sentences.

1 play video games

→ **I also love to** play video games.

2 play tennis with my friends

→ _____

3 play soccer with my brother

→ _____

D Look at the pictures and complete the sentences.

1 (science)

→ **My favorite subject is** science.

2 (art)

→ _____

3 (P.E.)

→ _____

+TIP

Subjects

English
Korean
math
social studies
history

E Look at the pictures. Complete the sentences with the words in the box.

astronaut	~~video game designer~~	athlete

💡 Use "an" when the job begins with a vowel (a, e, i, o, u).

1 **I want to be a** video game designer.

2 _____

3 _____

Sentence Practice ^{Plus}

A Read the short paragraph. Correct the mistakes and rewrite the sentences.

My name is Anna Jones. I'm in the <u>four</u> grade at West Elementary School. I like <u>read</u> comic books and play board games. I want to <u>being</u> an athlete.

_____

_____

_____

_____

B Look at the picture and read the conditions. Introduce yourself as if you are Ryan Winters like A above.

Conditions

① Write four sentences.

② Include the following information:
grade (3), Baker Middle School / sing, play the guitar / singer.

③ Include "like to."

_____

_____

_____

_____

Brainstorming

Introduce yourself. Complete the graphic organizer. Use the ideas in Collecting Ideas or come up with your own.

My Name Is _____	
Age and Grade	• •
My Hobbies	• • •
My Favorite Subject	
My Dream	• •

❧ **More Hobbies**

decorate cakes / write stories / do Taekwondo / listen to music / play the piano

❧ **More Jobs**

doctor – help sick people / veterinarian – take care of animals / chef – open a restaurant
artist – draw comic books / teacher – teach English to children / actor – star in movies

First Draft

Complete the first draft by using the graphic organizer.

Title	_____
Introduction	Hello, let me _____ myself.
Body	
Age	My name is _____. I'm _____ old,
Grade	and I live _____. I'm _____ grade at
My Hobbies	_____ School. I like to _____
	_____ and _____ in my free time. I also
My Favorite Subject	love _____. My favorite subject is
My Dream	_____. I want to be _____.
	I want _____ someday.
Conclusion	
	Thank you for listening.

Unit 2
This Is My Family

Writing Goal   Write about your family.

Type of Writing   Descriptive Writing » Introduction

Descriptive writing describes a person, place, or thing. It shows what the person, location, or object is like.

Before You Write

A **Read and answer the questions.**

1 Do you have a big family?

☐ Yes, I do. ☐ No, I don't.

2 How many people are in your family?

My family has _____ members.

3 What does your mom like to do?

She likes to _____ .

B **Fill in the chart with the words in the box.**

chef	quiet	teacher	smart
kind	doctor	noisy	vet

Jobs	Personalities
• _____	• _____
• _____	• _____
• _____	• _____
• _____	• _____

Understanding the Model Text

A **Read the model text and answer the question.**

My Family

My family has five members. My mom is a chef and is very smart. She likes to bake on the weekends. My dad is quiet and likes to read books. He teaches math at a high school. My sister is in kindergarten. She is noisy and likes to play outside. My grandmother is old, but she is energetic. She is good at playing tennis. My family likes to walk in the park together. We are a very happy family.

Q What is the passage mainly about?
  a. what the family likes to do together
  b. what the family members are like

B **Read the model text again and complete the graphic organizer.**

My Family	
Mom	• job: _____ • personality: very smart • hobby: likes to _____ on the weekends
Dad	• job: _____ at a high school • personality: _____ • hobby: likes to read books
Sister	• education: in _____ • personality: noisy • hobby: likes to _____
Grandmother	• personality: old, but she is _____ • good at: playing _____

C **Complete the paragraph by using the model text.**

Title	My Family

Introduction

My family has _____ members.

Body

Mom
- job / personality
  / hobby
Dad
- personality
  / hobby / job

My mom is _____ and is _____. She likes

to _____. My dad is _____ and likes to

_____. He _____.

Sister
- education /
  personality / hobby
Grandmother
- personality
  / good at

My sister is _____. She is _____ and likes

to _____. My grandmother is old, _____

she is _____. She is good at _____. My

family likes to _____ together.

Conclusion

We are a very happy family.

Collecting Ideas

Look at the example. Fill in the blanks with the words and phrases in the box.

funny	~~jog~~	do magic tricks
friendly	play outside	paint pictures

1

- mom
  - active
  - ___jog___ every day

2

- dad
  - _____
  - tell jokes

3

- brother
  - kind / _____
  - help others

4

- sister
  - noisy
  - _____

5

- grandfather
  - energetic
  - _____

6

- grandmother
  - quiet / shy
  - _____

Sentence Practice

Ⓐ Look at the pictures and complete the sentences.

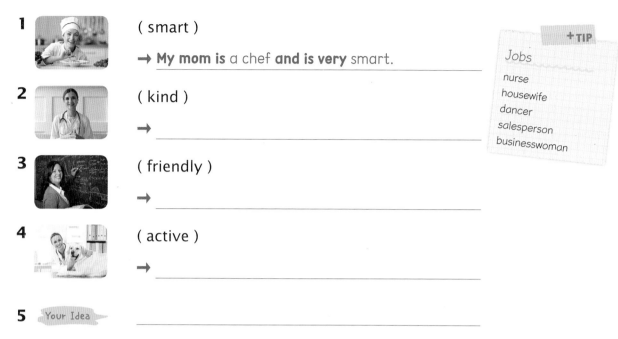

1 (smart)

→ **My mom is** a chef **and is very** smart.

2 (kind)

→ _____

3 (friendly)

→ _____

4 (active)

→ _____

5 Your Idea _____

+TIP

Jobs

nurse
housewife
dancer
salesperson
businesswoman

Ⓑ Look at the example and complete the sentences with the phrases in the box.

play outside	help others
jog every day	tell jokes

1 She is noisy _____ **and likes to** play outside _____.

2 He is funny _____.

3 She is active _____.

4 He is kind _____.

5 Your Idea _____

C Look at the example and complete the sentences.

> (teach / math / high school)
> → **He teaches** math **at a** high school.

1 (work / car company) → _____

2 (work / hospital) → _____

3 (teach / P.E. / middle school) → _____

D Look at the example and rewrite the sentences.

1 My grandmother is old. She is energetic.

➡ My grandmother is old, **but** she is energetic. _____

2 My grandfather is retired. He is very active.

➡ _____

3 My grandmother is short. She is very strong.

➡ _____

E Look at the example and complete the sentences.

💡 Remember to write "verb-ing" after "be good at."

1 she / play tennis

➡ She **is good at playing** tennis. _____

2 he / do magic tricks

➡ _____

3 she / dance

➡ _____

Sentence Practice ^{Plus}

A **Read the short paragraph. Correct the mistakes and rewrite the sentences.**

My mom is a vet and is very friendly. My dad <u>work</u> at a bank. My brother <u>is</u> elementary school. My grandfather is old, <u>or</u> he is very active. He is good at <u>play</u> soccer.

_____

_____

_____

_____

B **Look at the picture and read the conditions. Introduce the family as if it is your own like A above.**

Conditions

① Write five sentences.

② Include the following information:
mom (teacher, very smart) / dad (hospital) / sister (high school) / grandmother (quiet, funny, paint pictures).

③ Include "but" and "be good at."

_____

_____

_____

_____

Brainstorming

Introduce your family. Complete the graphic organizer. Use the ideas in Collecting Ideas or come up with your own.

Mom	• job: • personality: • hobby:
Dad	• job: • personality: • hobby:
Brother / Sister	• education: • personality: • hobby:
Grandfather / Grandmother	• personality: • good at:

More Personalities

gentle / talented / creative / helpful / mean / rude / generous / cool

First Draft

Complete the first draft by using the graphic organizer.

Title

_____

Introduction

My family has _____.

Body

Mom
- job / personality
  / hobby
Dad
- personality
  / hobby / job

My mom is _____ and is _____. She likes _____. My dad is _____ and likes to _____. He _____.

Brother / Sister
- education /
  personality / hobby

My _____. _____ is _____ and likes _____. My

Grandfather /
Grandmother
- personality
  / good at

_____ is _____, but _____. _____ is good at _____.

My family likes to _____ together.

Conclusion

We are a very happy family.

Unit 3

Join Our Club

Writing Goal	Write about a school club.
Type of Writing	Persuasive Writing Notice
	Persuasive writing encourages a reader to make a choice by providing evidence and examples.

Before You Write

A **Read and answer the questions.**

1 What club are you a member of?

I'm in the _____ club.

2 How often does your club meet?

My club meets ☐ once ☐ twice ☐ three times   a week.

3 What club do you want to join?

I want to join the _____ club.

B **Match the pictures with the correct phrases in the box.**

drama club	dance club	art club
swim club	computer club	juggling club

1

_____

2

_____

3

_____

4

_____

5

_____

6

_____

Understanding the Model Text

A Read the model text and answer the question.

Join the Dance Club

Are you looking for an exciting club? Learn to dance! At the dance club, we learn how to breakdance, do ballet, and belly dance. Dancing is exciting and fun. We meet twice a week and learn new dances. We also shoot videos and post them on YouTube. Once a year, we have a dance contest for the whole school. Come to the gym after school on Mondays and Wednesdays.

Q What is the passage mainly about?
a. introducing the dance club
b. tips for learning to dance

B Read the model text again and complete the graphic organizer.

The Dance Club	
What We Learn	how to _____, do ballet, and belly dance
What We Do	• meet _____ a week and learn new dances • _____ and post them on YouTube
Special Event	have a dance contest _____ a year
Where and When	• the gym • after school on _____ and Wednesdays

C Complete the paragraph by using the model text.

Title	Join the Dance Club

Introduction

Are you looking for _____ club? Learn to _____!

Body

What We Learn

At the _____ club, we learn how to _____

_____. _____ is _____.

What We Do

We meet _____ a week and _____.

We also _____.

Special Event

_____ a year, we _____ for the

whole school.

Conclusion

Where and When

Come to _____ after school on _____

_____.

Collecting Ideas

Look at the example. Fill in the blanks with the phrases in the box.

act, sing	juggle bean bags	draw, paint
~~belly dance~~	use computer programs	float, swim

1

- The Dance Club
- breakdance, do ballet, and

  belly dance

2

- The Juggling Club
- _____, balls, and rings

3

- The Art Club
- _____, and make things

4

- The Computer Club
- _____

5

- The Drama Club
- _____, and dance on a stage

6

- The Swim Club
- _____, and dive

Sentence Practice

A **Look at the example and complete the sentences.**

(breakdance, do ballet, and belly dance)
→ **We learn how to** breakdance, do ballet, and belly dance.

1 (juggle bean bags, balls, and rings)

→ _____

2 (draw, paint, and make things)

→ _____

3 (float, swim, and dive)

→ _____

4 (act, sing, and dance on a stage)

→ _____

Your Idea

5 _____

B **Look at the pictures. Complete the sentences with the words and phrases in the box.**

doing art   swimming   dancing   acting

1 **Dancing is** exciting **and** fun. _____ (exciting / fun)

2 _____ (relaxing / fun)

3 _____ (exciting / interesting)

4 _____ (refreshing / relaxing)

C **Look at the example and complete the sentences.**

💡 Use "once, twice, three / four times" when writing about the number of times.

1 (2 / learn new dances)

We meet twice a week and learn new dances.

2 (1 / learn about art)

_____

3 (3 / prepare for the school play)

_____

D **Look at the example. Complete the sentences with the phrases in the box.**

| post them | shoot videos | hang them |

1 We _____shoot videos_____ and post them on YouTube.

2 We shoot videos and _____ on our Facebook page.

3 We draw cartoon characters and _____ on the wall.

E **Look at the example and rewrite the sentences.**

💡 Start with a verb when you give advice or tell someone to do something.

1 Come to the gym. Come after school on Mondays and Wednesdays.

→ Come to the gym after school on Mondays and Wednesdays.

2 Come to Room 13. Come after school on Fridays.

→ _____

3 Come to the swimming pool. Come after school on Wednesdays and Fridays.

→ _____

36

Sentence Practice ^{Plus}

A **Read the short paragraph. Correct the mistakes and rewrite the sentences.**

At the drama club, we learn how to <u>acting</u>, sing, and dance on a stage. We meet three <u>time</u> a week and prepare for the school play. <u>Coming</u> to the auditorium after school.

_____

_____

_____

B **Look at the picture and read the conditions. Write a notice for the computer club like A above.**

Conditions

① Write three sentences.

② Include the following information:
use computer programs / practice typing and coding / computer room.

③ Include "how to + verb" and "once / twice / three times."

_____

_____

_____

Brainstorming

Write about a school club. Complete the graphic organizer. Use the ideas in Collecting Ideas or come up with your own.

Join the _____	
What We Learn	
What We Do	• •
Special Event	
Where and When	• •

✦ **More School Clubs**

science club / cooking club / Taekwondo club / English club / soccer club / music club

First Draft

Complete the first draft by using the graphic organizer.

Title _____

Introduction Are you looking for _____ club? Learn to _____

_____!

Body

What We Learn At the _____ club, we learn how to _____

_____. _____ is

What We Do _____. We meet _____ a week

and _____. We also

_____.

Special Event _____ a year, we _____

for the whole school.

Conclusion

Where and When Come to _____ after school _____

_____.

Unit 4

I Like
My New Room

Writing Goal	Write about your room.
Type of Writing	Descriptive Writing » Email
	Descriptive writing describes a person, place, or thing. It shows what the person, location, or object is like.

Before You Write

A **Read and answer the questions.**

1 Do you have your own room?

☐ Yes, I do.   ☐ No, I don't.

2 What color are your walls?

My walls are _____ .

3 What is in your room?

There is / are _____ in my room.

B **Fill in the chart with the words in the box.**

desk	pillow	lamp	bed
carpet	dresser	bookshelf	blanket

Furniture	Accessories
• _____	• _____
• _____	• _____
• _____	• _____
• _____	• _____

Understanding the Model Text

A **Read the model text and answer the question.**

To : emily000@mail.com
Subject : **My New Room**

Hi, Emily,

My family is moving to a new house. This is what my new room looks like. It has yellow walls and a white ceiling. It feels calm and peaceful. There is a desk under the window. I write in my diary there. My bookshelf is next to the door. My bed is across from the window. It has a brown blanket and yellow pillows on it. My favorite lamp is next to my bed. I'm so excited!

Your friend,

Anne

Q The topic sentence is the main idea of the passage.
Underline the topic sentence.

B **Read the model text again and complete the graphic organizer.**

My New Room	
Colors	_____ walls and a _____ ceiling
Feeling	calm and _____

Furniture and Accessories	• desk: _____ the window
	• _____ : next to the door
	• bed: _____ the window
	  - a brown blanket and yellow _____ on it
	  - my favorite _____ is next to it

42

C **Complete the paragraph by using the model text.**

Title	My New Room

Introduction

Hi, _____,

My family is moving to a new house. This is what my new room

_____.

Body

Colors / Feeling

It has _____ walls and a _____ ceiling. It feels

Furniture and
Accessories

_____ and _____. There is a _____

_____. I _____ there. My

bookshelf is _____. My bed is _____

_____. It has _____

_____ on it. My favorite _____ my bed.

Conclusion

I'm so excited!

Your friend,

_____

Collecting Ideas

Look at the example. Fill in the blanks with the words and phrases in the box.

on	over	between	across from
~~next to~~	under	behind	in front of

1

- My bookshelf is ___next to___ the door.

2

- My bed is _____ the dresser.

3

- My teddy bear is _____ the bed.

4

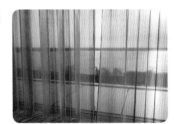

- My curtain is _____ the window.

5

- My guitar is _____ the bed.

6

- My bookshelf is _____ the desk.

7

- My chair is _____ the window.

8

- My desk is _____ the bed and the bookshelf.

Sentence Practice

A **Look at the pictures. Complete the sentences with the phrases in the box.**

a blue carpet	~~a white ceiling~~
a purple carpet	orange walls

1 It has yellow walls and _____a white ceiling_____ .

2 It has white walls and _____ .

3 It has a white ceiling and _____ .

4 It has a white ceiling and _____ .

5 Your Idea _____

B **Look at the example and complete the sentences.**

(calm / peaceful)
→ **It feels** calm **and** peaceful.

1 (calm / relaxing)

→ _____

2 (cheerful / warm)

→ _____

3 (comfortable / quiet)

→ _____

Your Idea

4 _____

C Look at the pictures. Complete the sentences with the words in the box.

over	under	next to	on

1 (desk)

There is _____ **a** desk under _____ the window.

2 (white curtain)

There is _____ the window.

3 (large bookshelf)

There is _____ the desk.

4 (small lamp)

There is _____ the desk.

D Look at the pictures. Complete the sentences with the words and phrases in the box.

bed	desk		between	in front of
teddy bear	bookshelf		on	across from

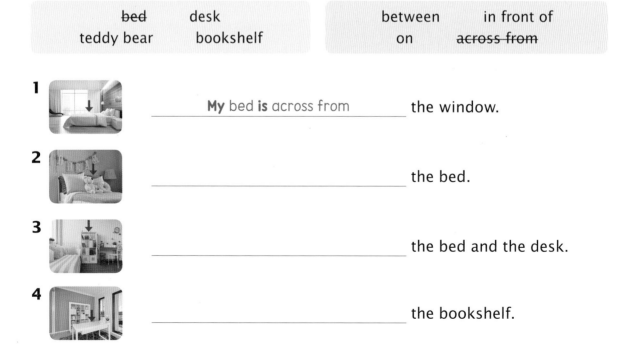

1 _____ **My** bed **is** across from _____ the window.

2 _____ the bed.

3 _____ the bed and the desk.

4 _____ the bookshelf.

Sentence Practice ^{Plus}

A **Read the short paragraph. Correct the mistakes and rewrite the sentences.**

This is what my new room <u>looking</u> like. It has blue walls and <u>white</u> ceiling. There is a small desk <u>next</u> the bed. My favorite lamp is <u>between</u> the desk.

_____

_____

_____

_____

B **Look at the picture and read the conditions. Write about the room in the picture like A above.**

Conditions

① Write four sentences.

② Include the following information: purple walls / ceiling / large bed – window / teddy bear.

③ Include "there is" and two prepositions.

_____

_____

_____

_____

Brainstorming

Write about your new room. Complete the graphic organizer. Use the ideas in Collecting Ideas or come up with your own.

Colors	
Feeling	
Furniture and Accessories	

- **More Accessories**

  clock / candle / picture frame / trash can / cushion

- **More Colors**

  silver / gold / beige / navy blue / peach / brown

First Draft

Complete the first draft by using the graphic organizer.

Title _____

Introduction

Hi, _____,

My family is moving to a new house. This is what my new room _____.

Body

Colors / Feeling

Furniture and Accessories

It has _____ and _____. It feels

_____. There is _____

_____. I _____.

My _____.

My _____.

It has _____.

My favorite _____.

Conclusion

I'm so excited!

Your friend,

_____

Unit 5

This Is My Best Friend

Writing Goal	Write about your best friend.
Type of Writing	Descriptive Writing » Journal

Descriptive writing describes a person, place, or thing. It shows what the person, location, or object is like.

Before You Write

A **Read and answer the questions.**

1 Do you have a best friend?

☐ Yes, I do. ☐ No, I don't.

2 What is your best friend's name?

His / Her name is _____.

3 What do you do with your friend?

We _____ together.

B **Match the pictures with the correct words and phrases in the box.**

| short hair | straight hair | tall |
| curly hair | freckles | thin |

1

_____

2

_____

3

_____

4

_____

5

_____

6

_____

Understanding the Model Text

A **Read the model text and answer the question.**

My Best Friend

This is my best friend, Liam. We spend a lot of time together. We skateboard together after school. We also study at a math academy together. Liam is smart, and he is interested in science. He has short brown hair and brown eyes. He is as tall as I am. Our friends think that we look like twins. I hope we can spend every day together.

Q The concluding sentence is the final thought of the passage.
Underline the concluding sentence.

B **Read the model text again and complete the graphic organizer.**

My Best Friend	
What We Do	• _____ together after school • _____ at a math academy together
What He Is Like	• _____ • interested in _____
What He Looks Like	• short brown hair and _____ • as _____ as I am • friends think that we look like _____

C **Complete the paragraph by using the model text.**

Title	My Best Friend

Introduction

This is my best friend, _____. We spend a lot of time

together.

Body

What We Do

We _____ together after school. We also _____

What He Is Like

_____ together. _____ is _____,

and _____ is interested _____.

What He Looks Like

He has _____ and _____.

He is _____ as I am. _____ think that

we look like _____.

Conclusion

I hope we can spend every day together.

Collecting Ideas

Look at the example. Fill in the blanks with the words and phrases in the box.

blond hair	~~short brown hair~~	long red hair	dark
thin	short curly hair	long straight hair	

1

- _____short brown hair_____ and brown eyes
- as tall as I am

2

- short brown hair and freckles
- as _____ as I am

3

- _____ and freckles
- hair is as long as mine

4

- _____ and green eyes
- as short as I am

5

- _____ and brown eyes
- hair is as curly as mine

6

- _____ and brown eyes
- hair is as _____ as mine

Sentence Practice

A **Look at the example and complete the sentences.**

(skateboard)
→ We skateboard **together after school**.

1 (play basketball)

→ _____

2 (go to dance class)

→ _____

3 (do homework)

→ _____

4 (go to our English academy)

→ _____

B **Look at the pictures. Complete the sentences with the words in the box.**

| sports | volunteer work | ~~science~~ | comedy |

💡 "Be interested in" is followed by a noun.

1 (smart)

Liam is _____ smart, **and he is interested in** science _____.

2 (outgoing)

Kyle is _____.

3 (funny)

Karen is _____.

4 (kind)

Jenny is _____.

5 Your Idea _____

C Look at the pictures. Complete the sentences with the words and phrases in the box.

~~short brown~~ long curly	freckles ~~brown eyes~~
short blond	blue eyes

1   He has _____short brown_____ hair and _____brown eyes_____ .

2   She has _____ hair and _____ .

3   He has _____ hair and _____ .

D Look at the example and complete the sentences.

💡 "As ~ as" is used to compare two objects, animals, or people.

1 | he / tall / I am | → He **is as** tall **as** I am.

2 | his hair / curly / mine | → _____

3 | she / thin / I am | → _____

E Look at the example and complete the sentences.

1 (our friends / twins)

→ Our friends **think that we look like** twins.

2 (some people / brothers)

→ _____

3 (my parents / sisters)

→ _____

56

Sentence Practice Plus

A **Read the short paragraph. Correct the mistakes and rewrite the sentences.**

This is my best friend, Karen. Karen is funny, and she is interesting in comedy. She have brown hair and freckles. Her hair is as longer as mine. My parents think it we look like sisters.

↓

_____

_____

_____

_____

B **Look at the picture and read the conditions. Introduce Sam as if he is your best friend like A above.**

Conditions

① Write five sentences.

② Include the following information:
friendly / robots / hair (blond, curly), eyes (green) / our teachers / brothers.

③ Include "as + adjective + as" and "that + subject + verb."

_____

_____

_____

_____

Brainstorming

Write about your best friend. Complete the graphic organizer. Use the ideas in Collecting Ideas or come up with your own.

What We Do	• •
What He / She Is Like	• •
What He / She Looks Like	• •

More Descriptions

wavy hair / wear glasses / chubby / cute / pretty

First Draft

Complete the first draft by using the graphic organizer.

Title _____

Introduction This is my best friend, _____. We spend a lot of time

together.

Body

What We Do   We _____ together after school. We also

_____ together. _____ is

What He / She Is Like   _____, and _____ is interested _____

What He / She Looks Like   _____. _____ has _____ and

_____. _____ is _____

as _____. _____ think

_____ we look like _____.

Conclusion

I hope we can spend every day together.

Unit 6
My Trip

Writing Goal   Write about your next trip.

Type of Writing   Narrative Writing   Letter

Narrative writing describes a story that happened to you. Narrative writing can also describe imaginary events.

Before You Write

A **Read and answer the questions.**

1 Do you like traveling?

☐ Yes, I do.   ☐ No, I don't.

2 Where did you go on your last trip?

I went to _____ .

3 Where do you want to go?

I want to go to _____ .

B **Match the pictures with the correct cities in the box.**

Beijing	New York	Cairo
Moscow	Sydney	Berlin

1

_____

2

_____

3

_____

4

_____

5

_____

6

_____

Understanding the Model Text

Ⓐ Read the model text and answer the question.

My Trip to Sydney

Dear Jill,

I'm going to visit Sydney with my parents in December. Sydney is famous for the Sydney Opera House. So, we are going to see it. We will also pet kangaroos and koalas at a wildlife park. We have one more exciting plan. My parents and I are going to Manly Beach. We are going to learn to surf. We'll have meat pies after we surf. I'm excited to go to Sydney!

Your friend,

Mark

Ⓠ The topic sentence is the main idea of the passage.
Underline the topic sentence.

Ⓑ Read the model text again and complete the graphic organizer.

My Trip to Sydney	
When	in _____
First Plan	• First: see _____ • Next: _____ and koalas at a wildlife park
Second Plan	• First: go to Manly Beach and learn _____ • Next: have _____ after we surf

C Complete the paragraph by using the model text.

Title	My Trip to Sydney

Introduction

Dear _____,

When

I'm going to visit _____ with _____ in

_____.

Body

First Plan

_____ is famous for _____. So, we are

going to _____. We will also _____

_____. We have one more exciting plan.

Second Plan

_____ going to _____.

We are going to _____. We'll _____

after _____.

Conclusion

I'm excited to go to _____!

Your friend,

_____

Collecting Ideas

Look at the example. Fill in the blanks with the phrases in the box.

~~pet kangaroos~~	see the flowers	watch the ballet
take a boat ride	see the old buildings	watch a musical

1

Sydney

- A Wildlife Park:

  _____pet kangaroos_____ and koalas

- Manly Beach: learn to surf

2

New York

- Central Park: have a picnic
- Times Square:

  _____

3

Cairo

- The Nile River:

  _____

- Khan el-Khalili Market:

  buy some souvenirs

4

Berlin

- Berlin Cathedral: take a tour
- Berlin Botanical Garden:

  _____

5

Moscow

- St. Basil's Cathedral: take photos
- Bolshoi Theater:

  _____

6

Beijing

- The Forbidden City:

  _____

- Silk Street Market: buy some crafts

Sentence Practice

A **Look at the example and complete the sentences.**

> Sydney / my parents / December
> → **I'm going to visit** Sydney **with** my parents **in** December.

> 💡 Use "be going to" to describe a future plan.

1 New York / my family / May

→ _____

2 Berlin / my cousins / April

→ _____

3 Moscow / my aunt and uncle / July

→ _____

Your Idea

4 _____

B **Look at the pictures and complete the sentences.**

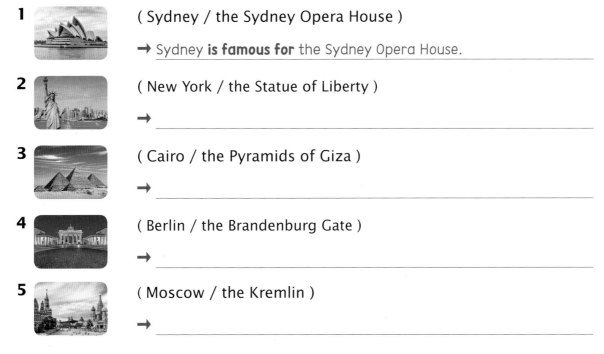

1 (Sydney / the Sydney Opera House)

→ Sydney **is famous for** the Sydney Opera House.

2 (New York / the Statue of Liberty)

→ _____

3 (Cairo / the Pyramids of Giza)

→ _____

4 (Berlin / the Brandenburg Gate)

→ _____

5 (Moscow / the Kremlin)

→ _____

C Look at the pictures. Complete the sentences with the phrases in the box.

have a picnic	~~pet kangaroos and koalas~~	take a boat ride

1 We will _____**pet kangaroos and koalas**_____ at a wildlife park.

2 We will _____ in Central Park.

3 We will _____ on the Nile.

D Look at the example and complete the sentences.

💡 Use "are" when the subject is plural and "is" when the subject is singular.

1 my parents and I / Manly Beach

→ My parents and I **are going to** Manly Beach.

2 my family / Times Square

→ _____

3 my cousins and I / the Berlin Botanical Garden

→ _____

E Look at the example and rewrite the sentences.

1 We will surf. Then, we'll have meat pies.

→ We'll have meat pies **after we surf**.

2 We will see the musical. Then, we'll have pepperoni pizza.

→ _____

3 We will shop. Then, we'll have roast duck.

→ _____

Sentence Practice Plus

A **Read the short paragraph. Correct the mistakes and rewrite the sentences.**

I'm <u>go</u> to visit Cairo with my parents in August. Cairo is famous <u>with</u> the Pyramids of Giza. We <u>is</u> going to the Khan el-Khalili market. We'll have Egyptian pancakes <u>after shop</u>.

_____

_____

_____

_____

B **Look at the picture and read the conditions. Write about your next trip as if you are going to Beijing like A above.**

Conditions

① Write four sentences.

② Include the following information:
aunt and uncle / October / the Great Wall / the Silk Street Market / roast duck / shop.

③ Include "be going to" and "after + subject + verb."

_____

_____

_____

_____

Brainstorming

Write about your next trip. Complete the graphic organizer. Use the ideas in Collecting Ideas or come up with your own.

My Trip to _____	
When	
First Plan	• First: • Next:
Second Plan	• First: • Next:

• **More Cities and Famous Places**

Paris – the Eiffel Tower / Rome – the Colosseum / London – Buckingham Palace / Bangkok – the Grand Palace

First Draft

Complete the first draft by using the graphic organizer.

Title

_____

Introduction

Dear _____,

When

I'm going to visit _____ with _____

in _____.

Body

First Plan

_____ is famous for _____.

So, we are going to _____. We will also _____

_____. We have one more exciting plan.

Second Plan

_____ going to _____.

We are going to _____. We'll

_____ after _____.

Conclusion

I'm excited to go to _____!

Your friend,

_____

Unit 7

Come to My Party

Writing Goal	Write an invitation to a party.
Type of Writing	Expository Writing ≫ Invitation
	Expository writing gives information about a topic or tells you how to do something.

Before You Write

A **Read and answer the questions.**

1 Do you like going to parties?

☐ Yes, I do.   ☐ No, I don't.

2 What is your favorite kind of party?

I like _____ parties.

3 What did you do on your last birthday?

I _____ .

B **Match the pictures with the correct words and phrases in the box.**

sleep	decorate	desserts
play games	swim	horror movies

1

_____ in a tent

2

_____ in a pool

3

_____ a tree

4

_____

5

eat some _____

6

watch _____

Understanding the Model Text

A **Read the model text and answer the question.**

Come to My Slumber Party

Dear Kylie,

I'm having a slumber party at my house next Friday. It starts at 6:00 P.M. I hope you can come. We will have pizza and watch movies. It will be fun! Can you bring a sleeping bag and a pillow with you? We will sleep in a tent in my backyard. Come and have fun at my slumber party!

Lisa

P.S. I'm also inviting Katie, Tanya, Michelle, and Debbie.

Q The topic sentence is the main idea of the passage.
Underline the topic sentence.

B **Read the model text again and complete the graphic organizer.**

My Slumber Party	
Where	at _____
When	_____ at 6:00 P.M.
What We Will Do	• have pizza and _____ • _____ in my backyard
What to Bring	a sleeping bag and _____

C **Complete the paragraph by using the model text.**

Come to My Slumber Party

Dear _____,

Where / When

I'm having _____ party at _____.

It starts at _____. I hope you can come. We will

What We Will Do

_____. It will be _____!

What to Bring

Can you bring _____ with you?

We will _____.

Come and have fun at _____!

_____

P.S. I'm also inviting _____.

Collecting Ideas

Look at the example. Fill in the blanks with the phrases in the box.

go trick-or-treating	~~bring a sleeping bag~~	bring a swimsuit
bring a gift	bring some food	take photos together

1

- Slumber Party
- have pizza and watch movies
- _bring a sleeping bag_ and a pillow

2

- Birthday Pool Party
- eat cake and play games
- _____ and a towel

3

- Potluck Party
- eat lunch and play badminton
- _____

4

- Christmas Party
- decorate a tree and eat cookies
- _____

5

- Halloween Party
- _____ and watch horror movies
- bring a costume

6

- Graduation Party
- play games and _____
- bring some snacks

Sentence Practice

Ⓐ **Look at the example and complete the sentences.**

> slumber party / at my house / next Friday
> → **I'm having a** slumber party at my house next Friday.

1 birthday pool party / at Cedar Swimming Pool / next Sunday

→ _____

2 Christmas party / at my house / on December 20

→ _____

3 potluck party / in my backyard / next Saturday

→ _____

Your Idea

4 _____

Ⓑ **Look at the pictures and complete the sentences.**

1 The slumber party starts at 6:00 **P.M.** _____

2 _____

3 _____

4 _____

5 Your Idea _____

C Look at the example and complete the sentences.

1 (have pizza) (watch movies)

→ **We will** have pizza **and** watch movies. _____

2 (go trick-or-treating) (watch horror movies)

→ _____

3 (decorate a tree) (eat cookies)

→ _____

D Look at the pictures. Complete the sentences with the phrases in the box.

| a swimsuit and a towel | ~~a sleeping bag and a pillow~~ | a costume |

1 **Can you bring** a sleeping bag and a pillow **with you?** _____

2 _____

3 _____

E Look at the pictures. Complete the sentences with the phrases in the box.

| a costume contest | ~~in a tent in my backyard~~ | in the big wave pool |

1 We will sleep _____ in a tent in my backyard _____ .

2 We will swim _____ .

3 We will have _____ .

Sentence Practice Plus

A **Read the short paragraph. Correct the mistakes and rewrite the sentences.**

I'm <u>have</u> a potluck party in my backyard next Saturday. It starts <u>in</u> 2:00 P.M. We <u>eat</u> lunch and play badminton. Can you <u>bringing</u> some food? We will have an eating contest.

_____

_____

_____

_____

B **Look at the picture and read the conditions. Write an invitation to a Christmas party like A above.**

Conditions

① Write five sentences.

② Include the following information:
my house / December 20 / 4:00 P.M. /
decorate, tree / eat cookies / exchange gifts.

③ Include the preposition "at" and "Can you ~?"

_____

_____

_____

_____

Brainstorming

Write an invitation to a party. Complete the graphic organizer. Use the ideas in Collecting Ideas or come up with your own.

Come to My _____	
Where	
When	
What We Will Do	
What to Bring	

❖ **More Parties**

New Year Party / Snack Party / Craft Party / Dance Party

❖ **More Places**

the game arcade / the playground / a restaurant / an amusement park

First Draft

Complete the first draft by using the graphic organizer.

Title _____

Introduction   Dear _____,

Body

Where / When   I'm having _____

_____. It starts at _____.

What We Will Do   I hope you can come. We will _____

_____. It will be _____!

What to Bring   Can you bring _____ with you?

We will _____.

Come and have fun at _____!

Conclusion

_____

P.S. I'm also inviting _____.

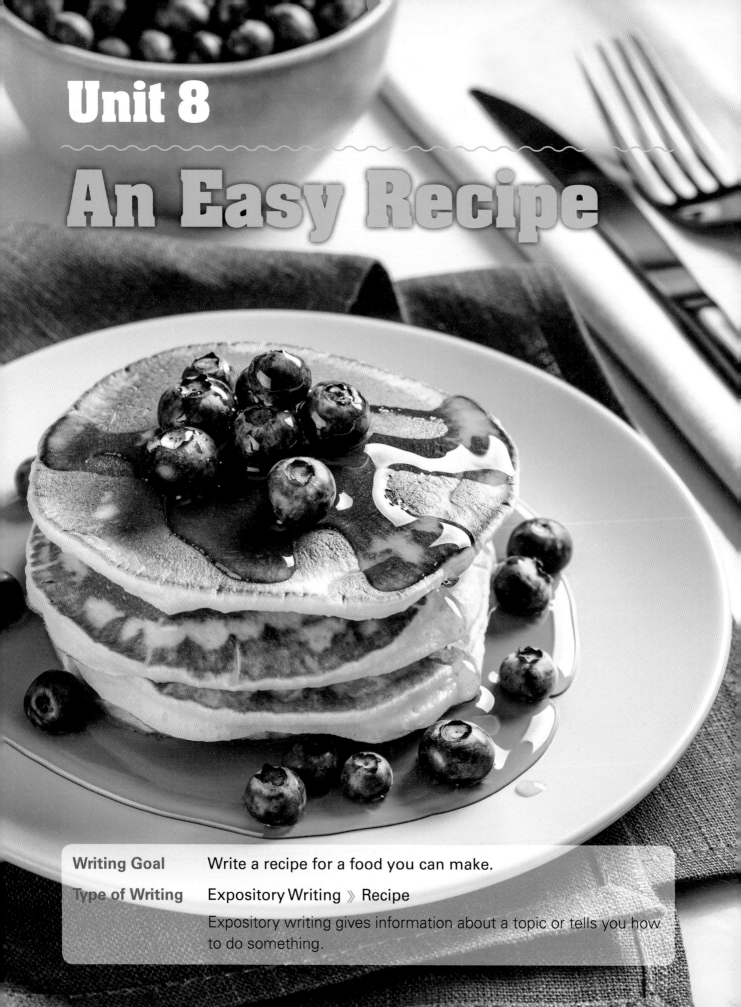

Unit 8
An Easy Recipe

Writing Goal	Write a recipe for a food you can make.
Type of Writing	Expository Writing » Recipe
	Expository writing gives information about a topic or tells you how to do something.

Before You Write

A **Read and answer the questions.**

1 Do you like to cook?

    ☐ Yes, I do.   ☐ No, I don't.

2 What food can you make?

    I can make _____.

3 What do you want to learn how to make?

    I want to learn how to make _____.

B **Match the pictures with the correct words in the box.**

stir	melt	pour
mix	boil	cook

1

2

3

_____

_____

_____

4

5

6

_____

_____

_____

Understanding the Model Text

A Read the model text and answer the question.

Let's Make Pancakes

How to make pancakes:

Do you want to make some pancakes? You will need milk, eggs, and pancake mix.

First, mix the pancake mix, milk, and eggs together.

Next, melt some butter in a pan and then pour some batter into the pan.

Then, cook the pancakes until they are fluffy.

Finally, add some syrup or fruit.

Enjoy your delicious pancakes!

Q What is the passage mainly about?
   a. pancake ingredients
   b. a pancake recipe

B Read the model text again and complete the graphic organizer.

Pancakes	
Ingredients	milk, eggs, and _____
First	_____ the pancake mix, milk, and _____
Next	• _____ some butter in a pan • _____ into the pan
Then	cook the pancakes until _____
Finally	add some _____

C **Complete the paragraph by using the model text.**

Title

Let's Make Pancakes

Introduction

How to make _____ :

Body

Ingredients

Do you want to make _____ ? You will need

_____.

First

First, _____.

Next

Next, _____ and then _____

_____.

Then

Then, _____ until _____.

Finally

Finally, _____.

Conclusion

Enjoy your delicious _____ !

Collecting Ideas

Look at the example. Fill in the blanks with the phrases in the box.

> chop the vegetables ⠀⠀ ~~pour some batter~~ ⠀⠀ ~~cook the pancakes~~
> boil the curry ⠀⠀ fry the rice ⠀⠀ mix the eggs and milk
> stir the eggs ⠀⠀ fry the meat and vegetables

1

Pancakes

- mix the pancake mix, milk, and eggs
- ___pour some batter___ into the pan
- ___cook the pancakes___

2

Scrambled Eggs

- _____
- pour the egg mixture into the pan
- _____

3

Fried Rice

- _____ and ham
- put the rice, vegetables, and ham in the pan
- _____

4

Curry

- chop the meat and vegetables
- _____ in the pan
- _____

Sentence Practice

A **Look at the pictures. Complete the sentences with the phrases in the box.**

| milk, eggs, pancake mix | rice, vegetables, ham |
| meat, vegetables, curry powder | two eggs, milk, butter |

1 **You will need** milk, eggs, **and** pancake mix.

2 _____

3 _____

4 _____

5 Your Idea _____

B **Look at the pictures. Complete the sentences with the phrases in the box.**

| mix the pancake mix, milk, | chop the meat |
| mix the eggs | chop the vegetables |

1 _____ **First,** mix the pancake mix, milk, _____ and eggs together.

2 _____ and milk with a fork.

3 _____ and ham.

4 _____ and vegetables.

C Look at the example and complete the sentences.

1 (melt some butter / pour some batter)

→ ___Next, melt some butter___ in a pan ___and then pour some batter___ into the pan.

2 (melt some butter / pour the egg mixture)

→ _____ in a pan _____ into the pan.

3 (pour some oil / fry the meat and vegetables)

→ _____ into a pan _____

in the pan.

D Look at the example and rewrite the sentences.

1 Cook the pancakes. They are fluffy. → Cook the pancakes **until** they are fluffy.

2 Stir the eggs. They are firm. → _____

3 Boil the curry. It is cooked. → _____

E Look at the pictures. Complete the sentences with the words and phrases.

| some syrup or fruit | hot rice |
| some salt and pepper | a fried egg |

1 (add)

Finally, add some syrup or fruit _____ .

2 (add)

_____ .

3 (top the rice with)

_____ .

4 (serve the curry with)

_____ .

86

Sentence Practice Plus

A **Read the short paragraph. Correct the mistakes and rewrite the sentences.**

Do you want to <u>making</u> some fried rice?

You will <u>needs</u> rice, vegetables, and ham.

First, <u>chopping</u> the vegetables and ham.

Then, fry the rice <u>after</u> it is hot.

_____

_____

_____

_____

B **Look at the picture and read the conditions. Write a recipe for curry like A above.**

Conditions

① Write four sentences.

② Include the following information:
meat, vegetables, curry powder / chop /
boil – cooked.

③ Include an imperative sentence and "until."

_____

_____

_____

_____

Brainstorming

Write a recipe for a food you can make. Complete the graphic organizer. Use the ideas in Collecting Ideas or come up with your own.

Let's Make _____	
Ingredients	
First	
Next	
Then	
Finally	

First Draft

Complete the first draft by using the graphic organizer.

Title _____

Introduction   How to make _____ :

Body

Ingredients   Do you want to make _____?

You will need _____.

First   First, _____.

Next   Next, _____ and then

_____.

Then   Then, _____ until _____.

Finally   Finally, _____.

Conclusion

Enjoy your delicious _____!

Vocabulary & Structure Review

Unit 1
Let Me Introduce Myself

Read the words and phrases. Write the meaning next to each word and phrase.

1	introduce		11	athlete	
2	live (*v.*)		12	video game designer	
3	grade		13	astronaut	
4	elementary school		14	model airplane	
5	middle school		15	comic book	
6	draw		16	science	
7	favorite (*a.*)		17	P. E. (= physical education)	
8	subject		18	Mars	
9	own (*a.*)		19	play board games	
10	someday		20	ride a bike	

Structures

1 in the + ordinal number + grade

e.g I'm <u>in the sixth grade</u> at Johnson Elementary School.

2 like [love] to + verb

e.g I <u>like to play</u> with my dog and draw pictures in my free time.
       I also <u>love to play</u> video games.

92

Unit 2
This Is My Family

Read the words and phrases. Write the meaning next to each word and phrase.

1	member		11	smart	
2	chef		12	quiet	
3	vet (= veterinarian)		13	shy	
4	weekend (↔ weekday)		14	noisy	
5	bake		15	energetic (= active)	
6	teach		16	friendly (= kind)	
7	jog		17	retired	
8	paint (*v.*)		18	joke	
9	math (= mathematics)		19	kindergarten	
10	personality		20	do magic tricks	

Structures

1 be good at + verb-ing

e.g She <u>is good at playing</u> tennis.

2 but + subject + verb

e.g My grandmother is old, <u>but she is</u> energetic.

Unit 3
Join Our Club

Read the words and phrases. Write the meaning next to each word and phrase.

1	join		11	post (v.)	
2	learn		12	contest	
3	breakdance (v.)		13	whole (a.)	
4	belly dance (v.)		14	float	
5	gym		15	dive	
6	exciting		16	juggle	
7	interesting		17	practice (v.)	
8	relaxing		18	play (n.)	
9	refreshing		19	do ballet	
10	shoot		20	look for	

Structures

1 how to + verb

e.g At the dance club, we learn <u>how to</u> breakdance, do ballet, and belly dance.

2 once / twice / three times

e.g We meet <u>twice a week</u> and learn new dances.

<u>Once a year</u>, we have a dance contest for the whole school.

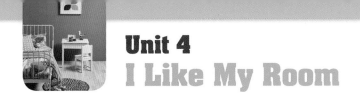

Unit 4
I Like My Room

Read the words and phrases. Write the meaning next to each word and phrase.

1	move		11	calm	
2	wall		12	peaceful	
3	ceiling		13	cheerful	
4	bookshelf		14	warm	
5	dresser		15	comfortable	
6	next to		16	behind	
7	across from		17	in front of	
8	blanket		18	between	
9	pillow		19	write in one's diary	
10	lamp		20	look like	

Structures

1 there is a / an + noun

e.g There is a desk under the window.

2 prepositions: next to, across from, on, etc.

e.g My bookshelf is next to the door.

My bed is across from the window.

It has a brown blanket and yellow pillows on it.

Unit 5
This Is My Best Friend

Read the words and phrases. Write the meaning next to each word and phrase.

1	spend		11	dark (*a.*)	
2	skateboard (*v.*)		12	mine	
3	academy		13	freckle	
4	together		14	outgoing	
5	short hair (↔ long hair)		15	hope (*v.*)	
6	curly hair (↔ straight hair)		16	every day	
7	blond hair		17	comedy	
8	thin (↔ fat)		18	volunteer work	
9	tall (↔ short)		19	do homework	
10	twins		20	be interested in	

Structures

1 as + adjective + as

e.g He is <u>as tall as</u> I am.

2 that + subject + verb

e.g Our friends think <u>that we look</u> like twins.

96

Unit 6
My Trip

Read the words and phrases. Write the meaning next to each word and phrase.

1	trip		11	musical (*n.*)	
2	visit		12	crafts	
3	parents		13	shop (*v.*)	
4	pet (*v.*)		14	souvenir	
5	wildlife park		15	cathedral	
6	beach		16	theater	
7	plan (*n.*)		17	botanical garden	
8	surf (*v.*)		18	have a picnic	
9	meat pie		19	be famous for	
10	roast duck		20	take a boat ride	

Structures

1 be going to + verb

e.g I'm going to visit Sydney with my parents in December.

2 after + subject + verb

e.g We'll have meat pies after we surf.

Unit 7
Come to My Party

Read the words and phrases. Write the meaning next to each word and phrase.

1	bring		11	pool (= swimming pool)	
2	sleeping bag		12	swimsuit	
3	tent		13	wave	
4	backyard		14	slumber party (= pajama party)	
5	invite		15	Halloween party	
6	snack		16	potluck party	
7	dessert		17	graduation party	
8	decorate		18	horror movie	
9	trick-or-treat (v.)		19	have fun	
10	costume		20	take photos	

Structures

1 preposition "at"

  e.g It starts <u>at</u> 6:00 P.M.

2 Can you ~?

  e.g <u>Can you</u> bring a sleeping bag and a pillow with you?

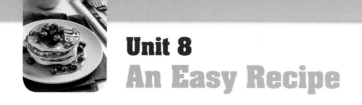

Unit 8
An Easy Recipe

Read the words and phrases. Write the meaning next to each word and phrase.

1	pour (v.)		11	serve	
2	mix (v., n.)		12	batter (n.)	
3	melt		13	pan	
4	cook (v.)		14	fluffy	
5	add		15	firm (a.)	
6	top (v.)		16	recipe	
7	stir		17	delicious	
8	chop (v.)		18	vegetable	
9	boil		19	mixture	
10	fry		20	salt and pepper	

Structures

1 imperative sentence

e.g First, <u>mix the pancake mix, milk, and eggs together.</u>

2 until + subject + verb

e.g Then, cook the pancakes <u>until they are</u> fluffy.

Memo

Memo

Memo

Memo

Essential Guide to Writing

Writing Avenue

Workbook

Paragraph Writing

1

DARAKWON

Essential Guide to Writing

Writing Avenue

Workbook

Paragraph Writing

1

DARAKWON

Unit 1 Let Me Introduce Myself

A **Look at the pictures and write the sentences.**

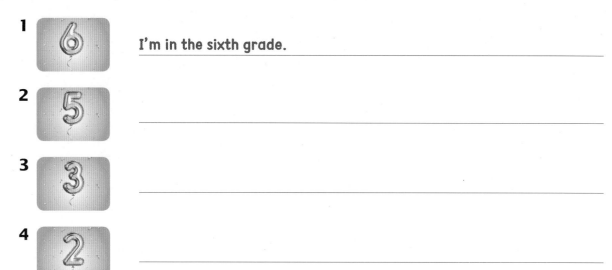

1   I'm in the sixth grade.

2   _____

3   _____

4   _____

B **Look at the example and unscramble the sentences.**

1   love / video games / play

→ I love **to** play video games.

2   like / tennis / play / with my family

→ _____

3   love / soccer / with my friends / play

→ _____

4   like / cakes and cookies / bake

→ _____

2

C Match the phrases. Then, write the sentences.

1	I also love	•	• subject is art
2	My favorite	•	• introduce myself
3	I want to be	•	• in Toronto
4	Hello, let me	•	• to play video games
5	I want to make	•	• a video game designer
6	I'm 12 years old, and I live	•	• my own games someday
7	I'm in the sixth grade at	•	• and draw pictures in my free time
8	I like to play with my dog	•	• Johnson Elementary School

1 _____

2 _____

3 _____

4 _____

5 _____

6 _____

7 _____

8 _____

Revise & Edit

Introduce yourself. Refer to the First Draft in the student book. Then, edit your paragraph.

Title	
Introduction	
Body	
Conclusion	

Editing Checklist ☐ Capitalization ☐ Punctuation ☐ Grammar ☐ Spelling

Final Draft

Write the final draft.

Title

Unit 2 This Is My Family

A **Look at the example and complete the sentences.**

1 grandmother / old / energetic

→ **My** grandmother **is** old**, but she is** energetic.

2 grandfather / quiet / funny

→ _____

3 grandmother / noisy / very cool

→ _____

4 aunt / thin / very strong

→ _____

B **Look at the pictures and complete the sentences.**

1 (play tennis)

She is good at playing tennis.

2 (do magic tricks)

_____

3 (dance)

_____

4 (bake bread)

_____

C **Match the phrases. Then, write the sentences.**

1	My family has	•
2	My sister is in	•
3	She is noisy and	•
4	My family likes to	•
5	He teaches	•
6	She likes to bake	•
7	My mom is a chef	•
8	My grandmother is old,	•

- kindergarten
- five members
- and is very smart
- on the weekends
- likes to play outside
- but she is energetic
- math at a high school
- walk in the park together

1 _____

2 _____

3 _____

4 _____

5 _____

6 _____

7 _____

8 _____

Revise & Edit

Introduce your family. Refer to the First Draft in the student book. Then, edit your paragraph.

Title

Introduction

Body

Conclusion

Editing Checklist ☐ Capitalization ☐ Punctuation ☐ Grammar ☐ Spelling

Final Draft

Write the final draft.

Title	

Unit 3 Join Our Club

A **Look at the example and complete the sentences.**

1 (dance club / breakdance, do ballet, and belly dance)

→ **At the** dance club, **we learn how to** breakdance, do ballet, and belly dance.

2 (juggling club / juggle bean bags, balls, and rings)

→ _____

3 (swimming club / float, swim, and dive)

→ _____

4 (drama club / act, sing, and dance on a stage)

→ _____

B **Look at the example and complete the sentences.**

1 once a year / have a dance contest

→ Once a year, **we** have a dance contest **for the whole school**.

2 twice a year / put on a play

→ _____

3 three times a year / have an art show

→ _____

4 once a year / put on a juggling show

→ _____

C **Match the phrases. Then, write the sentences.**

1	Learn to	•	•	and fun
2	We also shoot	•	•	dance
3	Are you looking	•	•	for an exciting club
4	Dancing is exciting	•	•	and learn new dances
5	We meet twice a week	•	•	a dance contest for the whole school
6	Come to the gym after	•	•	videos and post them on YouTube
7	At the dance club, we learn	•	•	school on Mondays and Wednesdays
8	Once a year, we have	•	•	how to breakdance, do ballet, and belly dance

1 _____

2 _____

3 _____

4 _____

5 _____

6 _____

7 _____

8 _____

Revise & Edit

Write about a school club. Refer to the First Draft in the student book. Then, edit your paragraph.

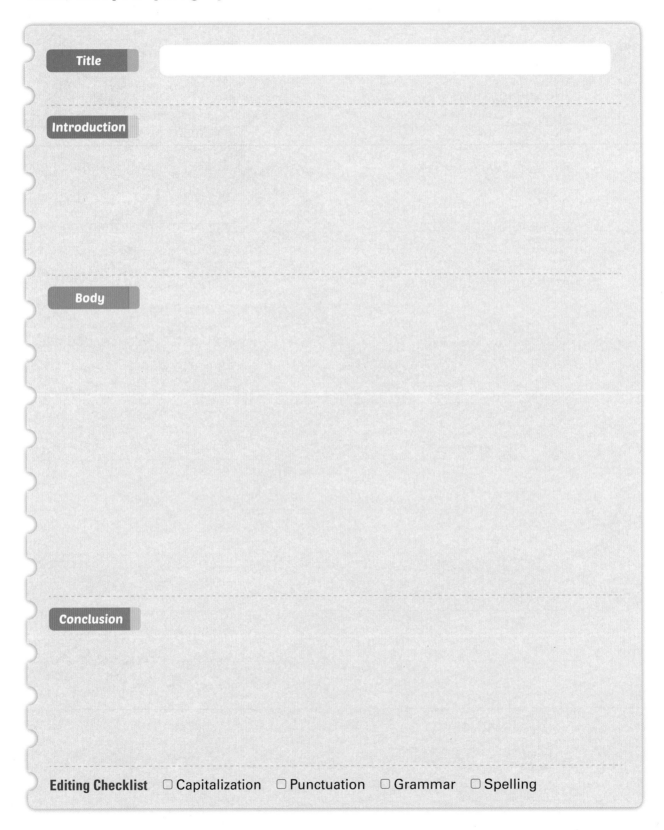

Title

Introduction

Body

Conclusion

Editing Checklist ☐ Capitalization ☐ Punctuation ☐ Grammar ☐ Spelling

Final Draft

Write the final draft.

Title	

Unit 4 I Like My New Room

A **Look at the example and complete the sentences.**

1 desk / under / window

→ **There is a** desk under **the** window. _____

2 blue curtain / over / window

→ _____

3 tall bookshelf / across from / bed

→ _____

4 large desk / next to / bookshelf

→ _____

B **Look at the pictures. Complete the sentences with the words and phrases in the box.**

in front of	next to	over	~~across from~~

1 (bed)

My bed is across from _____ the window.

2 (curtain)

_____ the window.

3 (bookshelf)

_____ the desk.

4 (desk)

_____ the bookshelf.

C **Match the phrases. Then, write the sentences.**

1 I write in   •   • looks like

2 It feels calm   •   • my diary there

3 My bookshelf is next   •   • from the window

4 My bed is across   •   • under the window

5 It has yellow walls   •   • to a new house

6 My family is moving   •   • and peaceful

7 There is a desk   •   • and a white ceiling

8 This is what my new room   •   • to the door

1 _____

2 _____

3 _____

4 _____

5 _____

6 _____

7 _____

8 _____

Revise & Edit

Write about your new room. Refer to the First Draft in the student book. Then, edit your paragraph.

Title

Introduction

Body

Conclusion

Editing Checklist ☐ Capitalization ☐ Punctuation ☐ Grammar ☐ Spelling

Final Draft

Write the final draft.

Title	

Unit 5 This Is My Best Friend

A **Look at the pictures and complete the sentences.**

1   (he / tall / I)

→ He **is as** tall **as** I **am**.

2   (her hair / long / mine)

→ _____

3   (she / thin / I)

→ _____

4   (his hair / curly / mine)

→ _____

B **Look at the example and rewrite the sentences.**

1   We look like twins.

→ **Our friends think that** we look like twins.

2   We look like brothers.

→ _____

3   We look like sisters.

→ _____

4   We look like cousins.

→ _____

C **Match the phrases. Then, write the sentences.**

1 He is as • • a lot of time together

2 We spend • • we look like twins

3 He has short brown hair • • spend every day together

4 We skateboard • • a math academy together

5 I hope we can • • is interested in science

6 We also study at • • together after school

7 Our friends think that • • and brown eyes

8 Liam is smart, and he • • tall as I am

1 _____

2 _____

3 _____

4 _____

5 _____

6 _____

7 _____

8 _____

Revise & Edit

Write about your best friend. Refer to the First Draft in the student book. Then, edit your paragraph.

Title	
Introduction	
Body	
Conclusion	

Editing Checklist ☐ Capitalization ☐ Punctuation ☐ Grammar ☐ Spelling

Final Draft

Write the final draft.

Title	

Unit 6 My Trip

A **Look at the example and complete the sentences.**

1 (learn to surf)

→ **We're going to** learn to surf. _____

2 (watch a musical)

→ _____

3 (see the flowers)

→ _____

4 (buy some crafts)

→ _____

B **Look at the example and complete the sentences.**

1 | surf → have meat pies |

→ **We'll** have meat pies **after we** surf. _____

2 | see the musical → have pepperoni pizza |

→ _____

3 | shop → have roast duck |

→ _____

4 | shop → have Egyptian pancakes |

→ _____

C **Match the phrases. Then, write the sentences.**

1	I'm excited to	•	• after we surf
2	We have one more	•	• go to Sydney
3	We are going	•	• to learn to surf
4	Sydney is famous	•	• exciting plan
5	I'm going to visit	•	• going to Manly Beach
6	My parents and I are	•	• for the Sydney Opera House
7	We'll have meat pies	•	• and koalas at a wildlife park
8	We will also pet kangaroos	•	• Sydney with my parents in December

1 _____

2 _____

3 _____

4 _____

5 _____

6 _____

7 _____

8 _____

Revise & Edit

Write about your next trip. Refer to the First Draft in the student book. Then, edit your paragraph.

Title	
Introduction	
Body	
Conclusion	

Editing Checklist ☐ Capitalization ☐ Punctuation ☐ Grammar ☐ Spelling

Final Draft

Write the final draft.

Title	

Unit 7 Come to My Party

A **Look at the pictures and write the sentences.**

1   It starts at 6:00 P.M. _____

2   _____

3   _____

4   _____

B **Look at the example and complete the sentences.**

1 | a sleeping bag / a pillow |

→ **Can you bring** a sleeping bag **and** a pillow **with you?** _____

2 | a swimsuit / a towel |

→ _____

3 | some food |

→ _____

4 | a costume |

→ _____

C **Match the phrases. Then, write the sentences.**

1	I hope	•	• 6:00 P.M.
2	It starts at	•	• you can come
3	Come and have	•	• watch movies
4	We will sleep in	•	• fun at my slumber party
5	I'm also inviting	•	• at my house next Friday
6	We will have pizza and	•	• a tent in my backyard
7	I'm having a slumber party	•	• and a pillow with you
8	Can you bring a sleeping bag	•	• Katie, Tanya, Michelle, and Debbie

1 _____

2 _____

3 _____

4 _____

5 _____

6 _____

7 _____

8 _____

Revise & Edit

Write an invitation to a party. Refer to the First Draft in the student book. Then, edit your paragraph.

Title

Introduction

Body

Conclusion

Editing Checklist ☐ Capitalization ☐ Punctuation ☐ Grammar ☐ Spelling

Final Draft

Write the final draft.

Title	

Unit 8 An Easy Recipe

A **Look at the example and rewrite the sentences.**

1 Can you melt some butter in a pan?

→ Melt some butter in a pan.

2 Can you chop the vegetables and meat?

→ _____

3 Can you pour some oil into a pan?

→ _____

4 Can you mix the eggs and milk?

→ _____

B **Look at the example and correct the mistakes.**

1 Cook the pancakes until <u>it</u> are fluffy.

→ Cook the pancakes until **they** are fluffy.

2 Stir the eggs until <u>it is</u> firm.

→ _____

3 <u>Frying</u> the rice until it is hot.

→ _____

4 <u>Boils</u> the curry until it is cooked.

→ _____

30

C **Match the phrases. Then, write the sentences.**

1	Enjoy your •	•	eggs, and pancake mix
2	Do you want to •	•	or fruit
3	Finally, add some syrup •	•	delicious pancakes
4	You will need milk, •	•	milk, and eggs together
5	Then, cook the pancakes •	•	make some pancakes
6	First, mix the pancake mix, •	•	until they are fluffy
7	Next, melt some butter in a pan and •	•	then pour some batter into the pan

1 _____

2 _____

3 _____

4 _____

5 _____

6 _____

7 _____

Revise & Edit

Write a recipe for a food you can make. Refer to the First Draft in the student book. Then, edit your paragraph.

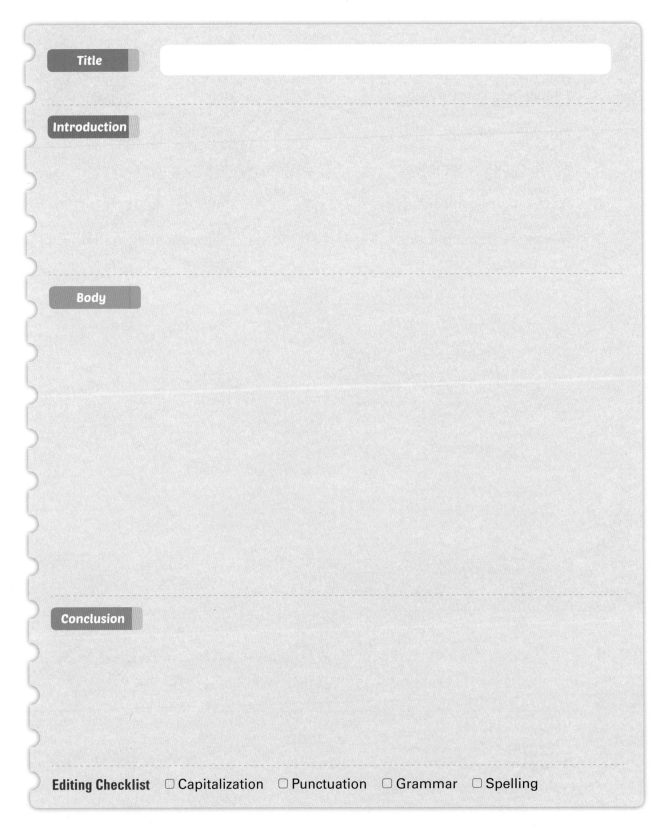

Title	
Introduction	
Body	
Conclusion	

Editing Checklist ☐ Capitalization ☐ Punctuation ☐ Grammar ☐ Spelling

Final Draft

Write the final draft.

Title

Memo

Memo

Memo